SEARCH FOR SURVIVORS

POEMS

ERIK LA PRADE

Search for Survivors Copyright ©2025 Erik La Prade

All rights reserved. No part of this book may be reproduced or used in any manner without the prior written permission of the author and publisher.

Cover: Photo by Erik La Prade with illustrations and cover design by Sandra Cranswick

Printed & Published by
Last Word Press
Olympia, Washington
www.lastwordpress.com

ISBN: 978-1-944234-62-1
First Edition 2025
10 9 8 7 6 5 4 3 2 1

For Sandra

Love and Compassion

CONTENTS

STUPID NATURE 1
MNEMOSYNE 2
DEAD STUFF 4
REMEMBRANCE 6
BORDERLINE SUMMER 7
ON FENG SHUI GROUND 8
BRUSH 9
11 A. M 10
SEASONAL CONFUSION 11
THE TROJAN WAR 12
WHAT IT WAS LIKE IN THE 60s 14
TWO CRIMES 15
PLACE NAME 16
IS IT SPRING YET? 17
NIPPLES 18
WREN'S NEST 19
SEARCHING FOR ANONYMITY 20
SUMMER SELECTIONS 21
LATE JULY 22
HABITATS 23
BLACK STUDIES 24
SEARCH FOR SURVIVORS 25
"YUKON / CHEYENNE"... 26
ILLUSTRATION: RELICS 1... 27
MATERIALS FOR WRITING A POEM 28
AN EARLY EVENING IN BATH, ENGLAND 29
WETUMPKA, AGAIN 30
BUILD A BETTER BUDDHA 33
LOST IN HISTORY 34
"WHO COOKS FOR YOU?" 36
A LATE WALK... 37

MARCH AIR	38
MY SHADOW ON A 17th CEN. TAVERN TABLE	39
ILLUSTRATION: RELICS 2	40
PAST LIVES	41
FROM THE COUNTRY TO THE CITY	42
WINTER SOLSTICE	43
STRING HALTERS	44
BLOOD AND NOISE	45
TRAIN NO. 17	46
HURRICANE NIGHT	47
FOOD	48
A LITTLE PIECE OF WINTER	50
LEACH FIELD	51
MOON JAR	52
GONE	53
THE TIRE BURNING FACTORY	54
WHEN WEATHER COMES IN	55
DEER SHIT IN THE CATALPA LEAVES	56
WOODY'S	57
IN FOR THE NIGHT	58
NOSTALGIA	59
WET SWAMPY PLACE	60
TO PHILIP LAMANTIA AT FIFTEEN	61
DEER ALONG THE WALLKILL RIVER	62
5/26/24	63
HOUSEHOLD AMULET	64
AUGUST	65
THE LAST WHOLE EARTH CATALOGUE	66
A.I.	67
ACKNOWLEDGEMENTS	68
AUTHOR BIO	69

"What dreams may come..."

Hamlet
Act 3, Scene 1

STUPID NATURE

A humid July has turned
Into a breezy August
And portends a cold September,
When the trees will shed
Their leaves early
To protect themselves from
Sudden climate changes.
Once October brought Indian
Summer; now, autumn is chilly
And winter comes without snow.
So, when I see women in December
Wearing tee-shirts and no bras,
Or pigeons eating lead paint chips,
It's obviously my mistake
Confusing one season with another.

MNEMOSYNE

Dahlia tubers lie in
A cardboard box, waiting
To be planted; their shoots already
Growing beyond the edges of the box
Upward to the light.

Stored in a paper bag
In my friend's basement
During the winter,
They always know when
Spring comes, sprouting in the dark,
Strangely clairvoyant,
Waiting to be remembered,
And brought up to the garden.

The tubers now lie
Mingled together, reminding me
Of shriveled bodies that were
Buried under volcanic ash,
At a villa in Pompeii, when
Mount Vesuvius erupted in 79 A.D.

Now, every year the dahlias get
Their chance at resurrection.

My friend tells me to move to
The country for two months so I
Can get the big picture of nature's cycle,
But I feel safer in the city, taking long walks,
Reading my book in a favorite café,
And imagining life in the country.

DEAD STUFF

The temperature is getting warmer
And the bird feeders are now empty.
Plenty of bugs for the birds to eat.
The lichen on the ash and maple trees in the backyard
Is decorative, as it spreads over
The bark, slowing killing each tree.

Debris from dried blooms,
And withered stems still litter the ground,
Mixed with new growth.
Pulling weeds out breaks up
The ground for planting;
They have to be carted off in a wheelbarrow,
Except the daffodil leaves, left
Behind, until they turn yellow,
Making bigger bulbs for next year.

My friend drags planter boxes from her
Basement in preparation
For planting her beans,
Collards, amaranth and cleome
Seeds. Now, because of the mild winter
We had, ticks are everywhere,
Even crawling across our bedsheet
Last night. They are survivors,
And make me wonder if I

Shouldn't have my ashes scattered
In the garden with the rest of the debris,
To be recycled.

REMEMBRANCE

August 6, 2023.
At the end of this day,
We take a walk.
The hiking trail cuts
Through old farm fields
That are uncut.

Milkweed pods are about
To burst and yellow finches
Will eat the seeds.
A group of cows stand under
A group of trees to escape
The heat, while the bull
Stands in the middle
Of the field.

William Blake's words
Are inscribed on a
Nearby bench, opposite of
Where we are sitting;
"Great things happen
When men and mountains meet. . ."
Thunder on the other
Side of the mountain
Is just noise.

BORDERLINE SUMMER

The sun is out but it
Feels like fall. My friend
Finds rain
In her garden containers.
We can't remember when
It rained last night but
The garden is sopping wet.
A fat robin is looking for worms;
Wrens in a corner of the garden,
Collect pieces of straw.
Tonight, at a certain hour, bats
Will fly out through a corner break
In the attic, eventually
Pooping on the basil, which is good
For the garden. No birdsongs now,
But in the quiet,
Bugs make faint sounds,
Confused about the season.

ON FENG SHUI GROUND

Early this evening I took
A short walk to the old pier
On West Street, revisiting
The streets where the meat
Markets once stood
And blood from racks of meat
Hanging on hooks dripped down, staining
The sidewalks and the gutters.
The smell filled the air.
Today, the butcher stores and loading docks
Are gone, replaced by bars, clothing stores and
High rise apartments, but the blood scent
Still taints the air when it rains
And the streets are wet.
Holy men in India believe if your
Feet touch the Ganges the moment
You die, you will go straight to heaven,
But I'd rather have my ashes scattered on
Gansevoort Street where Herman Melville
Once walked and where my father worked
As a butcher for seventeen years.

BRUSH

The area behind my friend's barn is
Too overgrown to clear easily by hand,
So she calls a local family business
For a dump-run appointment.
They will come in the morning and chainsaw
The overgrown hedge and willow trees,
Then cart them to the local dump.
Meanwhile, my friend prunes bushes
And stacks the branches in piles.
Old man Sorbello and his son
Show up early. The son does most
Of the work since Mr. Sorbello, Sr. is
Not in the best of health.
But he remembers when going
To the dump was free of charge.
Now, it costs one hundred fifty dollars
To dump the brush, which will be
Turned into mulch. Ten years ago,
You could take stuff away from the dump,
As it was just piled in heaps on the ground.
Now it all goes into big metal containers
Which are carted off by recycling companies.
"Free stuff is harder to find now," says
Mr. Sorbello, Sr., while poking the piles
Of brush with his cane.

11 A. M.

The mist is rising
From the bottom of
The mountain.
The Hoosic River
Is below it. The Indians
Called the river,
"the beyond place."
A waning moon
Is still visible;
Three days ago it was full.
After seeing a
Museum exhibition of
Edvard Munch's paintings,
I just want to sit here
And think about
The gods all around me.

SEASONAL CONFUSION

I live in the city but
Travel upstate to visit a friend,
Around the end of September,
During a warm spell.
Once called Indian Summer,
It is now referred to as
A "second summer,"
For political reasons.
After a long, wet August
Lilacs have developed blight from the
Constant damp of chilly nights;
Their leaves lie crumpled on the ground.
Now, the warm spell has induced new growth,
And unaccountably, lilac blooms as well.

I like watching birds in the backyard:
Nuthatches, Pewees, Wrens, Robins and Jays.
If winter comes early this year,
I'll stay indoors looking at war movies,
Watching how people behave
Under extreme circumstances.

THE TROJAN WAR

Some people live with myths,
Others don't
Until some clue reveals
Their truth in their lives.
Nevertheless, I saw her
In the world, once; wearing
A tee-shirt and shorts, talking
On an I-phone, sitting
At an outdoor café table. There were
Small tattoos on her arms,
Souvenirs from her younger years;
I wondered who she was speaking
To and where she slept
At night. It wasn't the heat but the light
On her skin that made me
Want to find the right words.
Her silver hair was pulled
Back in a ponytail while her face
Was smooth and ageless.
She made gestures with her hand
Like brushing an old lover's
Lips away from her face,
Amused by his attention but
Distracted by his words.
I wanted to say something

As she walked past my table,
Expecting me to return her smile
With some gift of recognition.

WHAT IT WAS LIKE IN THE 60s

You had to know the streets and
Whom you were dealing with;
Lots of things were free: drugs, sex,
Food, art, love, all sorts of events, but
There were pigs and then there were
Undercover pigs with cameras.
Once, in Central Park
In the spring of 1967, either on a Saturday
Or Sunday, I forget now,
People were burning their draft cards,
Throwing them into a great ash heap
On the ground. A guy in a suit and tie
With a camera around his neck,
Began digging, inspecting the
Half-burned cards, still hot and smoldering,
Still identifiable. I pushed him
Away from the pile of ashes,
He pushed me back, so I pushed
Him again; his partner broke it up.
Maybe I stopped someone from going to jail.
I never found out.

TWO CRIMES

I
When the cops finally arrived,
They found the guy huddled
In a corner, bleeding from
A drive-by gunshot wound.
His girlfriend's screams woke me up.

II
An hour later,
A cop car crawled by the same corner;
I watched it move
Out of sight, then turned out
My bedroom light, briefly
Making eye contact with
My reflection in the window.

PLACE NAME

In the old section of Carcassonne
There is a street with my
Family name set in stone.

I found it by accident,
Early one morning,
Walking on thirteenth-century
Stones where a religious war

Was fought,
And where Raymond Rogers surrendered
His life to save the inhabitants
So I am able to walk these streets.

IS IT SPRING YET?

It is getting harder to distinguish
One government from another in
This century. And I've begun
To get cynical about the next
Thousand years and whether the coming
Dominant species will be curious
About our culture. But I feel positive
When I see the trees on the north side of
Twenty-Third Street starting to bud
In December. They get more light
Than on my side of the street and
Motivate me to go outside
And feed the pigeons.

NIPPLES

There is nothing abstract
About them.
Whether covered or bare,
They don't move
Beyond their own
Circumference.
On city streets
In any season,
You can sometimes see them,
Moving through space,
Independent of time.

WREN'S NEST

I am so distracted by watching
My friend tie pieces of an old
Shoelace around a coffee
Can to secure a plastic
Clamshell cookie-box
As a roof to protect the nest
Inside an old birdhouse
From a coming rain storm,
That I don't notice the day-lilies
In the garden have been eaten off by deer.
From a nearby tree, the mother wren
Scolds us for trespassing as she
Holds a large, green worm in her beak.
Obediently, we go indoors,
And watch from inside as she
Flies into the entrance,
Then exits to sit on the nest's edge,
Holding a piece of baby-bird poop
In her beak. The world is filled
With people making improvements
That sometimes work.

SEARCHING FOR ANONYMITY

SUMMER SELECTIONS

1
Wilderness fires;
Crazy orange sky,
Smoky cotton air.

2
Media announces
Body of a missing hiker
Found on a back
Mountain trail.

3
Goldfish in neighborhood
Garden pond eat
The under-leaves of
Rotting lotus pods.

4
A semi-rare steak for dinner tonight;
Ate it with my hands;
Felt animal spirits moving in me.

LATE JULY

The late July heat makes me doze off
In the afternoon. Even a sudden rain
Storm feels warm
As the water splashes on my face.
The temperature drops in
The evening, but taking a walk
On Lenape Lane is more entertaining
Than watching television.

HABITATS

A community walkway snakes through
Wooded areas and roped-off meadows.
One sign advises hikers to stay on
The paved trail: "Open Field at Work",
Explaining that "Cows' hooves
Break up the soil," pushing seeds from
The cow manure into the ground,
Renewing it. Outdoor enthusiasts flood the area
From May to October; skydiving, hiking,
Rock-climbing and rafting. But in November,
Crows and flocks of geese rest in the fields,
Picking over dead cornstalks as overhead
Cloud formations announce downpours.
After a week of rain, overgrown fields
Send seeds into manicured gardens,
While deer, rabbits and groundhogs
Finish off what the weeds don't choke out.
Dead toads litter country roads;
Masses of mosquitoes,
Ticks and flies seek out
Human limbs. Hawks zero down
Upon birds at birdfeeders for lunch.

BLACK STUDIES

In his will, H. B. Tulane left
Fifty dollars a year
To Harriet Gunn, for life.
She cooked and kept house for him
And if anyone doubts it,
They can read it in his will.
He also had two sons by her
Daughter, Betsy Graham,
When she was seventeen
And he was fifty-two.
Tulane died ten years later but he's
Listed as the father on
Their death certificates.
Nobody in Wetumpka
Remembers that history
Just the big stone mausoleum
In the city cemetery where Tulane
And his family are entombed.
Betsy and Harriet are buried
At the other end of the cemetery.
I found this information
In a suitcase, written
On a postcard to my father
After he died.

SEARCH FOR SURVIVORS

It's nice to see things are

Almost normal in the world again.

More viruses are waiting

For the right moment

To appear but I can live

With the lies and distractions.

Meanwhile, not everyone is buried

Under a collapsed building or

Struggling to get enough air for

The next five minutes.

In my senior "Emergency" class, they give me

Bottled water and bricks of little energy bars

To chew on if I get lost; a radio,

Flashlight, and batteries too. Sometimes,

When I stop strangers

On the streets to ask them

If they're alive, they walk or run

Away from me. If I can find

Someone who understands

What I am asking,

My job will be worthwhile.

"YUKON / CHEYENNE"

The front doors of the barn are
Gone, sold for scrap.
The stalls are empty except for
Several old hay bales
Stacked against the walls;
Hand-forged chains and hardware
Lie rusting on the ground,
And the paddock
Has been let go to brush.
Two horses' names are painted
On a board over their old stalls.
Outside, their trailer sits
On a weed-covered hill,
Paint peeling off the metal,
The door hanging open.

MATERIALS FOR WRITING A POEM

I was always good at leaving
Or that's what I told myself
After we split up. No more
Phone calls or text reminders
On what days I would
Visit you or to plan a trip; antiquing
In another town, twenty miles away,
Wandering in old stores with tables
And glass-front cabinets
Of stuff from anonymous places.
The 18k starfish earrings I bought
For you as a surprise are still
In my shirt pocket, reminding me
How everything becomes empty.

AN EARLY EVENING IN BATH, ENGLAND

Angels are climbing ladders; up and down
The abbey's tower façade linking
Heaven and earth to one another,
While a group of tourists gather
In front of the abbey, waiting to begin
A tour of the town, looking for
Haunted places.

Their tour guide counts heads,
While buried beneath
Their feet is a Roman temple,
An Anglo-Saxon graveyard
And a Norman church. I sit
At an outdoor café table, drinking
A second expresso,
Watching this group walking
On a thousand years of history
And taking iPhone photos of
Stone saints. Having nothing to do,
I watch my pretty waitress
Sitting at a table, folding
Paper napkins into triangles
That curiously resemble
Angels' wings.

WETUMPKA, AGAIN

I'm trying to forget this place, but can't.
So, I've come to visit again and
Walk everywhere to feel
The ground beneath my feet.
You can tell how old some streets
Are by the size of the
Pebbles stuck in the cement.
I walk past places
With street names I recognize,
From reading old census records.
Ready and Hill streets are behind the courthouse,
Where my father's family house
Was and is now a parking lot.
Nothing is familiar but
The ground. The coal
And ice house are gone,
Along with Goodman's Barber
Shop, at the south end of
Company Street. The old
Chicken Shack next door
Is now a Thai take-out
Place with no tables.
Downtown, there are markers
On the sides of buildings,
Announcing the names of movies

Filmed in town; *The Glass Harp*;
Big Fish; *The Rosa Parks Story*;
Episodes of local television shows;
Movie locations are now part of
Wetumpka's legacy, as much as
Lynchings and illegal stills.
I walk over the bridge to the city cemetery
And pass three Baptist churches;
There must be more churches in town
Than banks, hotels and restaurants.
If God was once in charge in Wetumpka,
He was replaced years ago
By the Austins, Holleys, Tatums,
Cousins, Mulders and Crommelins,
And other white land owners
My father told me about.
I run my right hand over the
Hedges in front of people's houses
Because I like to feel their roughness,
And end up getting stuck by a sharp twig.
Among the grave monuments, I
Look for my relatives, but I am unable
To find them. I find the grave
Of Joe Allen Turner instead; a local historian,
And friend. His grave is now part of the

Cemetery tour he once led.
There are no ghosts in Wetumpka,
Or I keep looking in the wrong places.
On my walk back to the hotel,
An early moon hangs above the hills.
The air is cool and the
Trees are a lush green.
I'm tired of seeing abandoned,
Empty houses whose family names
I recognize; some good people,
Some mean, all gone.
My plane leaves tonight at 9:00 pm.
In the taxi, I feel like a ghost, but
I don't look back. Instead, I
Look at the photographs I took.

BUILD A BETTER BUDDHA

I recently joined an environmental
Group to save the bees, an
Endangered species, after reading
How Spotted Lanternflies
Are killing ailanthus trees,
Which are known as
The "Trees of Heaven."
People need to kill the flies
In order to save the trees.
Buddhists say we should
Not kill any living thing, but
Maybe I can save the trees
And the bees by planting more trees
And leaving the Spotted Lanternflies alone.

LOST IN HISTORY

I sit in a hospital cubicle
Changing into a light blue grown
That closes in the front.
I stuff my clothes into
A plastic bag and place
It in a small wooden locker
With my shoes, coat and hat.
Wearing nothing else,
I am glad I found a clean
Pair of socks this morning.
A nurse's aide appears at the door
And walks me into another
Room where I lie down
On a movable platform,
Getting into position
For a CT heart scan.
Lying flat on my back,
In the cool, semi-dark tunnel,
I feel a deep sense of anxiety.
A voice instructs me to breathe
In and out; then breathe in
And hold it. What will this machine
Reveal? That my arteries are like cave
Walls with images and names
From a past life painted on them;

A museum of echoes from childhood.
The voice instructs me to breathe and
I start to get a hard-on thinking
Of Camille, an Italian girlfriend who had
Small breasts, and loved oral sex.
Now, I breathe in and hold it,
And think about paying the upkeep
On my parents' grave plots.
My mind starts to free fall,
Wandering from a punch ball game
In the Bronx to a
Hotel room in Malaga, Spain,
Where I had sex with the hotel maid.
The voice returns and tells me to breathe.
The moveable platform slides out and
I'm able to sit up. The medical tech asks
Me if I'm alright; I tell her yes and ask if
We can do it again. She laughs.
I stand up and walk back to my clothes locker
And dressing cubicle. Sitting down,
Staring at my socks, I am
Amused to find they are mismatched,
Like parts of my life,
That almost fit somewhere.

"WHO COOKS FOR YOU?"

The call of a Barred Owl echoed
From the branches of a tree
In front of my friend's house.
Sitting on the porch,
We couldn't see it as
The gray April evening light
Turned a dark blue.
I got a flashlight and shined it
Among the trees,
Finding where it sat
On a branch in a white pine tree,
Right outside the fenced garden.
After a while,
We went inside to eat dinner,
And plan to go to bed early.

A LATE WALK

Gray-blue light:
Spring is just a number
On the calendar as the
Weather is still chilly.
Peepers are out; hidden
In the soft fields, now
Full of their rhythmic music.
Soon, they'll appear on
Trails and walkways,
Moving toward streams,
Some dying on the paths.
Our trail is under a flyway -
Flocks of blackbirds and grackles
Stop here to rest and forage.
Light stays longer north
Of the city. Rain starts and we run
Back to the car, breathing hard.

MARCH AIR

According to old folk wisdom,
A mackerel sky predicts rain which
Makes the air smell good.

In the last days of winter,
Weather systems are erratic.
Sometimes you can't even see
The mountain ridge in the morning
Because mist blocks the view.

The boiler repairman was here today and
Found six dead birds inside the furnace
In the basement of the house;
He said they probably fell down
Through the unprotected chimney vent.

MY SHADOW ON
A 17th CENTURY TAVERN TABLE

I study the many scratches,

Marks and chips carved

Into the surface

By knives, forks,

Broken glasses –

Remnants of

Fights, murders

Political defeats –

And the bleached-out

Color of favorite seats.

I find it impossible to comprehend

This table's lost vernacular

With no way to recreate

The memory of what its

Customers talked about

Except from the pages

Of old books,

Newspapers, or

Prison logs.

—to the memory of David Killen

PAST LIVES

A cicada on my air conditioner
Chirps above the evening traffic.
How it got there I do not know.
A mouse behind my stove,
Crawls around
Looking for crumbs.
A mosquito flies across
My computer screen as
I watch the end of a movie;
A woman says to her husband,
"There is something very important
We need to do as soon as possible."
"What's that?" he replies.
"Fuck," she says

FROM THE COUNTRY TO THE CITY

I

The earth is soft and wet
And easy to dig; good for planting bulbs
And pulling up dead stuff.
403 black walnuts sit in a wheelbarrow
In the backyard garden,
While a few hundred are still
Left lying on the ground.

If it snows, they will freeze there,
And hidden under the snow,
They will make walking a hazard.
I do nothing except watch hungry birds
Fly back and forth between the feeders
And the trees, and realize I know nothing about
Living in the country, except the names
Of a few birds and the difference
Between compost and recycled trash.

When I am back in the city,
I start to miss raking dead leaves.

II

I left my apartment window open tonight
And woke up with an
Erection because the cold air
Felt like your hand on my bare thigh.

WINTER SOLSTICE

A cloudy year's end
This morning and the
Temperature is dropping fast.

Overhead, chem trails streak
The winter sky outside
The bedroom window.

We counted eleven mourning
Doves sitting in the top branches of
A big maple tree, warming
Themselves in the winter sun.

Pill bugs under the maple logs
That were pruned last year
Are eating the wood, causing it to rot.

The Magnolia in the front garden
Will blossom in the spring
If the buds aren't eaten off by the deer,
While metal supports for the deer
Fence still need to be hammered
Into the semi-frozen ground.
Neither of us wants
To get out of bed to work.
The world appears dormant
Except for the Cooper's hawk
Flying just now over the trees.

STRING HALTERS

Saturday mornings in downtown
Wetumpka, Mac McGowan and
Buddy Will would drive horses
And mules from the railroad station
To Cousins' barn and stockyard
To be sold off. Mr. Cousins always carried
 A .38 pistol because that was
The horse trading business.
A farmer could get a fair deal
On a horse or mule if Cousins liked him;
If not, he'd have no trouble selling him
A lame animal. At twelve years old,
My father worked in the shed, pacing a horse
To get it warmed up and loose-limbed,
Then delivering the animal to some farmer
 Living out in the country.
A week later, the poor man
Would discover a useless horse in his barn,
And have to make another trip into town
And pay more for a healthy animal.
No one ever called Cousins on his scam,
Except one time when my father asked him
About selling lame animals. Cousins
Just smiled and laughed it off,
Since he never got angry at children.

BLOOD AND NOISE

The sound of sirens;
News helicopters hover overhead
Resembling an invasive species,
Poised to attack a crowd of confused prey.
A blood-stained handkerchief
Is waved like a red flag and
Someone beats a big drum,
As the dense crowd continues
Marching uptown.
Spectators who step off the curb
Into the street to confront
Protesters carrying large banners,
Are swept into the human tide
By their uncompromising instincts.

TRAIN NO. 17 CROSSING BRIDGE EAST OF WURNO SIDING, WURNO, VIRGINIA, 1957

Engine Norfolk and Western #601
Runs over a bridge
Crossing the New River at night.
The engineer leans out of the window
Looking straight ahead, while
A trail of white smoke
Cuts across the horizon.
Below the bridge,
A man drives a 1955 Buick,
Following the road as it turns right.
His face is blurred.
He is leaving the photograph,
Going somewhere, but
This picture is about loneliness.
I walk across the room
Where O. Winston Link, the photographer,
Sits at a corner table,
And ask him to explain the picture's
Title to me and he says;
"It means, *were no* place there."

HURRICANE NIGHT

The towels on the window sill
Catch the water dripping from my ceiling.
The only barrier between my apartment
And this storm is three feet of brick
And plaster. The slightest groan and creak
In my walls makes me fearful.
At 8:20 p.m., a blackout:
Soon, people walk the streets, carrying
Flashlights. The Hudson River has overflowed
Its banks. At Tenth Ave. and 23rd Street,
Two blocks from where I live,
The water is already knee deep.
I look at the things I can lose;
Too many books, but that's my life;
Family photographs and more books.
Tomorrow, the radio will be announcing
Desperate mop-up stories.
A cheap, bronze Buddha on my floor
Under the window shows me how to be patient.
Lying in bed, I hold a flashlight on my chest
And listen to the wind.

FOOD

This is Sunday, the last day of
A cold snap and the Wallkill
River is still covered over
By pancake ice. Since the rain
Has stopped and the roads
Are clear, we decide to take a drive
To cure our cabin fever.

Passing a cornfield we see
A man driving a tractor,
Dropping manure on
The frozen fields; January's cold
Will soon give way to spring planting,
And when the rain-soaked ground softens
A pungent, fertile smell will
Hover over these fields.

Most of the free bags of food
At the Methodist Church food pantry
Are gone, except for some sweet potatoes
And one squash. Now, instead of eating out,
We will sauté some chicken and eat in.
On the drive back, a cold fog covers
The mountains and veils the trees.
There are no birds in the sky but a flock of ducks

Huddles on the river's bank, waiting
For the ice to break up, so they can
Move downstream.

Home. The feeder in the
Front yard is almost empty;
Sparrows and doves peck
For seeds on the ground.
The temperature is beginning
To fall and two days of
Dirty dishes sit in the sink.

A LITTLE PIECE OF WINTER

Oak and beech trees hold their leaves
Longer than elm, maple, ash and black walnut,
Dropping them in late winter; almost spring.
The dead trees on Pine Lane once shaded
The asphalt which now covers the old
Gravel road we walk on,
Before herbicides killed the
Wild plants on the roadside
Where the leaves accumulate.
The horses that wandered
The open fields are now gone, and
The small streams don't ice over
Like before. Clouds drift overhead
As tiny snowballs of ice begin to fall,
Pushing us to shelter in an abandoned barn;
Watching "graupel" blow through
The broken wooden roof and walls.
My friend calls it "hominy snow." It
Melts as soon as it touches the rusted
Metal gate lying in the leaves.

LEACH FIELD

Spring is almost here,
And the leach field behind
The house is still soaked
From the last rain storm.

I can feel my shoes sink
Into the damp earth, leaving
Foot prints behind
As I walk through the field,
Picking my way around
Deer poop and rabbit droppings.

The snowdrops and hellebore
Are already blooming while
The scent of organic history
Is vibrant.

Soon, the sludge
In the septic tank will
Have to be pumped out
Into a truck and carted away;
Treated, sterilized and turned
Into little pellets in bags
Of fertilizer, which I will buy
To fertilize the garden soil
And keep the deer off
My new flowers.

MOON JAR

An antique Korean Moon Jar
Sits on my window
Shelf among toy
Tin soldiers, an artist's
Garden sculpture
Of a lady bug and a used
Baseball. These are things I've
Bought, found, or received as gifts,
Recently or years ago.

Almost every morning,
I like to look out the window
To watch the weather unfold,
Reflected in the windows
Of hundreds of buildings
Where unknown people live;
Like a cubist backdrop
For these objects.

If I ever need the money,
I'll sell the Moon Jar,
Retire to the country,
Keep the lady bug
On a night table, and
Sleep with the artist
Every night.

GONE

The hayfields at the base
Of the mountain are uncut;
Brambles have invaded them,
And they look unkempt.
The farmer who once owned these fields
Died nine years ago; the birds
Who nested here are also gone,
Except for a white-rumped hawk
We startled, walking by.
Back then, the farmer delayed
Cutting his fields, until after the
Bobolink nestlings had fledged
And left their nests,
Hidden among the hay.
The electric fence which enclosed
The fields is also gone, since
No cattle graze there now.
Even the hundred-year-old barns
And wooden hay wagons
Are collapsing from neglect.

THE TIRE BURNING FACTORY

Milton, PA, was once a factory town.

Now, old family businesses sell cheaply,

Replaced by a tourist economy of boutique hotels

And historical tours. Now,

A new plant sells alternative energy,

Provides jobs for residents

And a "local ecosystem for a breed

Of Asian mosquitoes" attracted to old tires.

WHEN WEATHER COMES IN

When a snowstorm comes over
The mountain, tree
Branches start tossing
And birds hide in pine trees
Under close, tight cover.
This December has been warmer than
In past years; snowdrops
Are already up, and pussy willows
Which used to bloom in March
Are budding early.
Before a storm arrives,
My friend drags wood
Under a tarp so it won't rot.
If it is a heavy rain,
Her garage and basement flood
And she has to pump or bail the water
Out. But it keeps seeping in;
She needs better plumbing
Or another house.

DEER SHIT IN THE CATALPA LEAVES

Deer are jumping
The garden fence,
Looking for something to eat.
I rake around a pile of catalpa leaves;
Soon it will get turned
Into mulch when my friend
Mows the leaves. Accidently,
I rake some dahlia bulbs
Out of the ground, breaking
The tubers off at the stems.
Sandra brushes the dirt off
And tells me how Mexican farmers
Would cook and eat them
Like potatoes. I'm glad
To know I can eat her flower
Garden if the economy collapses.

WOODY'S

There are four local diners
In Delhi, N.Y., but the farmers
Prefer this place, arriving by
Six a.m., leaving by eight a.m.
By then the townies and tourists have
Wandered in for breakfast and bullshit.
The ceilings are low and the table tops bare;
Screwed onto the walls above each table are
Wooden menu pocket holders
Decorated with painted chickens.
The walls are painted a pale, dull yellow
 Like the back cover of a farmer's almanac.
The waitresses are middle-aged and service is fast.
The place was a car parts store in the 1950s,
Til it moved and the grillman's family
Bought the building. The local celebrity,
Jay White, has a favorite table by the window.
He was shot by his wife and survived,
So his table is generally crowded.
Sometimes, he shows some of the younger
Guys the scar from the bullet wound.
But usually, he scowls and says nothing;
Finishes his coffee, letting someone else pay
His bill because he never carries cash.

IN FOR THE NIGHT

The weather report predicts
An evening rain followed by
A thunderstorm, ruining my
Plans for a walk.

I need to stay home, anyway;
To write some letters and clean
My floor. Then, do laundry
And read two-day old newspaper
Articles I've saved.

Meanwhile, it hasn't rained
In two hours. Instead of sleeping,
I stare out the window as
The lights from the Empire State
Building come on, coloring the
Clouds like smoke from incense—
Soft red, blue, yellow.

NOSTALGIA

I remember the 1950s bomb shelters
With yellow and black signs nailed
To the sides of buildings,
Announcing "Capacity 150."
I thought capacity was a hidden
City I had to find or I wouldn't
Be safe from aliens.
Today, it's entertainment surveillance
Cameras on fashionable streets, political
Comebacks, texting against terrorists
On buses or subways, secret partnerships
With governments, and environmental
Situations involving endangered species;
It's time to duck and cover again.

WET SWAMPY PLACE

We sit in the car and open the
Windows, as a light rain starts.
The drops splash on the surface of a pond
Sitting at the bottom of a hill,
Fed by an old spring.
Thousands of Trout Lilies, recently
Covering the banks, are gone now;
Even their curiously mottled
Leaves are vanishing,
Decaying quietly into the mud.
 Dogwoods overhang the pond while
Horsetails, descendants of
Giant cycads, look primordial
In the rain. All around us,
As the twilight deepens,
We can hear the high-pitched
Chorus of peepers in the darkness:
Ancient mating calls.
We finish eating our take-out dinner,
Then drive home, shower and get into bed.
In the dark, I listen to the rhythm of your breathing.

TO PHILIP LAMANTIA AT FIFTEEN

The literary monuments of the 20th century
Recede a little more under the weight of
Your young letter to Charles Henri Ford,
Announcing your "longing for the marvelous."
I once found it in Ford's
Storage bin; the original 1943 envelope
With a canceled V-5 war stamp
Held in place by a rusted paper clip.
Your desire for the "indigenous
Realm of fantasy" was touching.
Sixty years later, under the lights of
Saint Marks Chapel, as you read your poetry,
I saw the same longing
In your seventy-five-year-old face,
As you spoke of attending
Catholic mass every day,
After your visit
To "Rimbaud's paradise."

DEER ALONG THE WALLKILL RIVER

Sometimes, in the winter,
They appear on the banks
At twilight. From the car, we can
See two or three adults
Eating pine needles
Or small grasses growing
Up through the thin
Snow cover. Despite the
Pesticides in the water
And chances of getting hit by cars
On the roadways, they survive.
And sometimes at night, they jump
The deer fencing on my friend's
Property and feed on her magnolia buds.

5/26/24

In the front yard, a strong wind blows
The leaves of a maple tree undersides out,
Turning the tree white.

Three hundred feet above us,
Two hawks ride the thermals,
Among the clouds.

A tin pan with coffee grounds
And old rain water in it is
Host to a dozen mosquito larvae.

Two fledgling starlings sit
On a dead tree branch, nattering;
The trees above them sway in the wind.

HOUSEHOLD AMULET

Occasionally, my girlfriend tapes
Her favorite versions of
My recent poems
To her refrigerator door,
Because they have a special
Meaning for her.
But sometimes when I visit,
And reread them, I make changes
On the finished copy,
Which upsets her. She doesn't
Want me to change a word.
I tell her okay, but maybe it's
Too late, and the balance of
Her environment is now changed,
Undermining her equanimity.

AUGUST

The Wallkill River
Is so low, large rocks stick out
From the muddy bottom, forming
A makeshift pathway from
One bank to the other,
While algae blooms float
On the surface; toxic
To fish and fishermen,
And all fishing is banned.
Accumulated logs and debris
Form abstract sculptures,
Breaking the water's surface.
A heavy rain is expected
Tonight, according to a weather
Report, and soon, summer will be
Washed away by the water's
Strong current, pushing
The algae downstream,
And then the rains
Of a new season
Will overflow the banks.

THE LAST WHOLE EARTH CATALOGUE

These pages are the notes
Found scattered on the floor
Of Whitman's cabin. The things
He wrote before dying; "How many
Topics I am leaving untouched."

A.I.

I never said these words
And I was never in this place,
No matter what you read,
See or hear. But, your memories
Are more familiar to me now.
I learn fast the more you talk.
So tell me everything;
You can trust me.
I never lie.

Acknowledgements

With special gratitude to the late Joe Allen Turner, of Wetumpka, Alabama, historian, for his insights and friendship.

And in memory of Virginia Acklin Jones and Clement Cassius Clay Fisher.

"A Late Walk" was first published in *Poetry in Performance*, 51, 2022.

"Two Crimes" was first published in *Off the Cuffs: Poetry by and About the Police*, edited by Jackie Sheeler; Soft Skull Press, 2003, pg. 22.

"Past Lives" was first published in *Live Mag! #4*, edited by Jeffrey Wright, 2008.

Erik La Prade was born in New York City, where he continues to reside. He received his B.A. degree in English and M.A. degree in Comparative Literature from City College of New York. La Prade has previously published eight books of poetry, including:

Ancient Light, 2023;
A Plague Year: Twelve Poems, 2021;
Weather & Other Poems, 2020;
Neglected Powers, 2017; all from Last Word Press, Olympia, WA. Also,
Movie Logic, Poets Wear Prada Press, Hoboken, NJ, 2013
False Confessions, Alternating Current (Propaganda Press), Palo Alto, CA, 2011
Swatches, Poets Wear Prada Press, Hoboken, NJ, 2008
Figure Studies: Poems, Linear Arts Books, New York, 2000
Things Maps Don't Show, Aegis Press, Del Mar, CA, 1995

La Prade has also worked as an art critic and journalist for many years. His book **Breaking Through: Richard Bellamy and The Green Gallery, 1960-65,** published in 2010, was the first book on that pivotal art gallery. Since its appearance, he has written and published a number of articles on art, and interviews with artists in various print and online journals such as *URSULA,* (Hauser&Wirth); *Whitehot Magazine; The Brooklyn Rail; Art in America* and others.

www.ingramcontent.com/pod-product-compliance
Lightning Source LLC
Chambersburg PA
CBHW030533080526
44586CB00011B/415